MAKE ME THE BEST

VOLLEYBALL PLAYER

BY JON ACKERMAN

SportsZone

An Imprint of Abdo Publishing
abdopublishing.com

abdopublishing.com

Published by Abdo Publishing, a division of ABDO, PO Box 398166, Minneapolis, Minnesota 55439. Copyright © 2017 by Abdo Consulting Group, Inc. International copyrights reserved in all countries. No part of this book may be reproduced in any form without written permission from the publisher. SportsZone™ is a trademark and logo of Abdo Publishing.

Printed in the United States of America, North Mankato, Minnesota
092016
012017

THIS BOOK CONTAINS
RECYCLED MATERIALS

Cover Photo: Nicholas Rjabow/Shutterstock Images, top left; Jimmy Mills/Shutterstock Images, top right; Shutterstock Images, middle left; David Porras/Shutterstock Images, bottom left; Michael Spomer/Cal Sport Media/AP Images, bottom right
Interior Photos: Nicholas Rjabow/Shutterstock Images, 4 (top); Shutterstock Images, 4 (middle); David Porras/Shutterstock Images, 4 (bottom); Michael Spomer/Cal Sport Media/AP Images, 4–5 (bottom); Jimmy Mills/Shutterstock Images, 4–5 (top); Michael Spomer/Cal Sport Media/Newscom, 7; Geoff Caddick/EPA/Newscom, 8; Matt Rourke/AP Images, 11, 21, 35; Jeff Roberson/AP Images, 13, 15; Sean M. Haffey/Getty Images, 16; Petr David Josek/AP Images, 19; Marc Serota/AP Images, 23; Christopher Halloran/Shutterstock Images, 24; Dave Martin/AP Images, 27; Marcio Jose Sanchez/AP Images, 29, 39, 43; Leo Correa/AP Images, 31; Newspix/Icon Sportswire, 32; Xinhua/Imago/Icon Sportswire, 37; Hailey Archambault/Icon Sportswire, 40; ZumaPress/Icon Sportswire, 45

Editor: Patrick Donnelly
Series Designer: Nikki Farinella
Content Consultant: Hugh McCutcheon, former head coach, USA Men's National Volleyball Team, USA Women's National Volleyball Team; current head coach, University of Minnesota women's volleyball team

Publisher's Cataloging-in-Publication Data

Names: Ackerman, Jon, author.
Title: Make me the best volleyball player / by Jon Ackerman.
Description: Minneapolis, MN : Abdo Publishing, 2017. | Series: Make me the best athlete | Includes bibliographical references and index.
Identifiers: LCCN 2016945434 | ISBN 9781680784923 (lib. bdg.) | ISBN 9781680798203 (ebook)
Subjects: LCSH: Volleyball--Juvenile literature.
Classification: DDC 796.325--dc23
LC record available at http://lccn.loc.gov/2016945434

TABLE OF

CONTENTS

INTRODUCTION

Volleyball players perform many different skills in a game. They need to move, jump, dive, and play the ball in various ways. During a single play, an athlete might dive for a ball and pass it to a teammate, scramble to her feet, race to the net, jump, and spike the ball.

Being able to do all these things at the right time takes a lot of practice. Those practiced skills are why volleyball is one of the most exciting and popular sports in the world.

Volleyball is different from many other sports because the movements it requires are not as simple as kicking a ball or throwing it in a hoop. The best volleyball athletes have great physical talents and abilities. They excel at the many skills that are necessary to become superstars. But they weren't born elite players. They had to work hard to become the best volleyball players they could be.

SERVE LIKE

JORDAN LARSON

ordan Larson stands about 15 feet behind the end line. She holds the volleyball with both hands in front of her waist. She bends over, looks down, and bounces the ball three times. Then, in one continuous motion, she stands tall again and tosses the ball with her right hand. It soars nearly 20 feet (6 m) in the air and a few feet in front of her.

Larson was the 2015 USA Volleyball Female Indoor Player of the Year.

As the ball reaches its peak and begins to drop, Larson takes three quick steps. Next she jumps off both feet. She swings her right arm above her head. At the top of her jump, her hand connects firmly with the ball. It rockets across the net.

Jordan Larson delivers a jump serve for Team USA.

The ball flies at an opponent's head. She ducks. Before she can turn around, the ball hits the court just inside the end line. It's another ace for Larson.

Larson helped the United States women's national team win the silver medal at the 2012 Olympic Games in London, England. It was Larson's first time representing her country in the Olympics.

SERVE LIKE JORDAN LARSON

- Work on tossing the ball first. Your goal is to toss the ball to the same place in front of your serving shoulder every time. You can't perfect your serve if you don't know where the ball will be as it comes down.

- Practice serving the ball to specific spots. Accuracy is an important factor to becoming a great server.

- Power up. Adding strength will help you add speed to your serves, making them even more difficult for your opponent to receive.

Larson knows a consistent toss is important to becoming a strong server.

Serving is important because it starts a game or rally. A bad serve can give the other team a point right away. But a good serve improves a team's chances of scoring.

Larson holds high school records in Nebraska for most career aces and most aces in one season. At the University of Nebraska, she led her team in aces every year. She graduated in 2009 with the university's career record for aces.

Her serving skills continued to shine with the US women's national team. In 2014 the US women's team won

LOGAN TOM

Logan Tom was just 19 years old when she made Team USA's roster for the 2000 Olympics. The four-time Olympian showed her serving skills in 2012 while playing for her professional team in Turkey. Taking the ball with a 15–9 lead, Tom performed her powerful jump serve an incredible 10 times in a row. She scored six aces during that span. Tom was following in the footsteps of Clay Stanley. He was named Best Server in the 2008 Olympics as he led the US men's team to the gold medal. Stanley is one of the most dominant servers in the sport's history.

Larson also stars as an outside hitter for Team USA.

the world championships for the first time. Larson served
more than anyone else on her team during the gold-medal
match against China.

Learning how to serve is necessary for every volleyball
player. A good serve improves a team's ability to defend
an attack. If a strong serve forces the other team into a
poor first pass, they are less likely to
mount a strong attack.

Larson has played professional volleyball in Puerto Rico, Russia, and Turkey.

Volleyball players use a variety
of different serves: underhand,
standing float, jump float, and overhand topspin serve.
Skilled players jump while serving. The most advanced
players take a running start before jumping.

A jumping float serve sends the ball over the net faster
than a standing float serve. It is also easier to control
than a jumping topspin serve. But a jumping topspin
serve creates the most power and speed. When hit hard,
the jumping topspin is the most difficult type of serve
to defend.

DRILL DOWN!

This drill will help you develop a more consistent serve.

1. Toss a ball in the air to a comfortable height and mark the spot where it lands on the ground.

2. Toss the ball up 50 times and see how close it lands to that spot. Repeat until the ball lands on the spot nearly every time.

3. Stand opposite a partner with the net between you. Serve back and forth from five different spots along the attack line.

4. When each player has successfully completed 10 serves, move

PLAY LIBERO LIKE

ERIK SHOJI

Liberos are primarily defensive specialists. Each team has one on the court at all times. You can spot liberos easily because they wear a different color jersey than their teammates. Liberos can only play in the back row, so they need to be outstanding at defense. They make big digs, receive serves, and pass to their teammates. And Erik Shoji is one of the best liberos in the world.

A dig happens when a player receives an opponent's attack and keeps the ball in play. Shoji made one of the most impressive digs of his career while playing for Stanford University. During a rally, one of the opposing team's attacks caught the

In college Shoji was the first men's volleyball player to be named first-team All-American four times.

Erik Shoji shows perfect form on this bump, or forearm pass.

Stanford team off guard. No one was at the net to block. An opponent had an uncontested spike. The ball zoomed to the middle of the court.

Shoji was in the back row. His momentum was carrying him to his left. But as the opposing player hit the ball, Shoji shifted to his right. He dove low to the ground with his right arm extended. Just before the ball touched the ground,

Shoji was named the Best Libero at the 2015 World Cup.

PLAY LIBERO LIKE ERIK SHOJI

- When receiving a serve, get in proper ready position: feet shoulder-width apart, knees bent, hips low, and arms in front of your body.

- Don't swing your arms at the ball. Instead, absorb the contact with your arms and control the ball.

- Improve the accuracy of your passes by pointing your thumbs in the direction you want the ball to go.

- Use one-armed or diving digs in emergency situations. The goal is simply to pop the ball up in the air and keep the point alive.

A one-armed dig is a last resort when you can't make a safer pass.

Shoji got his hand under it for an incredible dig. Stanford wound up winning the point.

Shoji has made great plays like that his entire career. At Stanford he set the national collegiate record with 1,402 career digs. After college Shoji joined the US men's national team. In 2014 he was the Most Valuable Player (MVP), Best Digger, Best Receiver, and Best Libero at a tournament involving teams from the North American region.

MISTY MAY-TREANOR

Misty May-Treanor is one of the best diggers ever. She won three Olympic gold medals in beach volleyball with her partner, Kerri Walsh Jennings. May-Treanor was shorter and quicker than her teammate. So she often played in the back, while Walsh Jennings blocked at the net. May-Treanor's digging skills earned her the honor of being named the best defensive player three times by the Beach Volleyball World Tour. No woman has received that award more often.

Misty May-Treanor was one of the best defensive players ever to set foot on a beach court.

A big dig can be a spectacular play. But making digs isn't the libero's only job. And liberos also aren't the only players who need to work on passing skills. Every player has to pass the volleyball at some point in a game. Besides digging, you can use a forearm pass or a set.

Standing just 6 feet tall, Shoji is proof that volleyball can be a game for shorter players, too.

A forearm pass is typically used to receive a serve. This is also called a bump. As a served ball heads toward you, bring your wrists and hands together. Your hands should be curled up in fists with your knuckles touching. Position your body directly behind the oncoming ball and bend your knees before the ball arrives.

With your arms straight, make contact just above your wrists. Your arms and upper body should remain still. You can angle your forearms in the direction you want the pass to go. Extend your legs and hips to help you make the pass. The goal of a pass is to send the ball to a teammate, who will then set the ball.

DRILL DOWN!

Play "pepper" to work on receiving and digging.

1. Stand 10 feet apart, facing your partner.

2. Toss a ball above your head and hit it toward your partner, who will dig the ball and direct it back to you.

3. Catch the ball and hit it again. You can change the speed of the hits to make the drill more challenging.

4. More advanced players can add another level to the drill: The player receiving the ball attempts to bump it straight up, set it to himself, and spike it back to his partner.

SET LIKE

PHIL DALHAUSSER

Phil Dalhausser is one of the most feared players in volleyball. He stands out from the crowd because he's 6 feet 9 inches tall and has a shaved head. He's an excellent hitter. He's an excellent blocker, too. He might be the best beach volleyball player in the world.

Opposing teams try to limit how much he touches the ball. In two-on-two beach volleyball, that means opponents mostly serve to his teammate. If his partner takes the first touch, Dalhausser then sets the ball on the second touch, and his partner hits on the third.

Dalhausser was the 2008 Olympic Beach Volleyball Most Outstanding Player. He won a gold medal with Todd Rogers.

This strategy forced Dalhausser to become an excellent setter, too.

Phil Dalhausser sets the ball as well as any player on the beach tour.

In 2015 Dalhausser and his partner, Nick Lucena, reached the finals of the Manhattan Beach Open. It's one of the biggest beach volleyball tournaments of the year. The opposing team served mainly to Lucena. On set point of the first game, Lucena bumped the ball high in the air. Dalhausser kept both eyes on it. He turned his body to the right, where Lucena was charging to the net.

The ball came down and briefly rested in Dalhausser's fingertips. Then in one smooth motion, he extended his

SET LIKE PHIL DALHAUSSER

- Get under the ball quickly. Keep your eyes on the ball as you move into position.

- For an overhead set, keep your arms up, elbows bent, and hands in front of your forehead until the ball hits your fingers.

- With your fingers spread open, make a diamond shape with your index fingers and thumbs, but keep your hands about an inch apart. This creates a spot for the ball to land.

- Extend your knees and elbows to send the ball up. End with your fingers pointing up.

Dalhausser bends his knees as he prepares to set the ball.

Dalhausser was the Beach Volleyball World Tour's Most Outstanding Player in 2010, 2013, and 2014.

arms and legs and set the ball back up in the air. It fell about three feet off the net, giving Lucena more than enough room. His spike zipped past the blocker and hit the sand just inside the line. Dalhausser and Lucena won that game, and they went on to win the match. It was their first Manhattan Beach Open title together.

Dalhausser probably would not say setting is his favorite skill. He also is a world-class hitter and blocker.

ALISHA GLASS

The two biggest tournaments in women's volleyball are the Olympics and the world championships. The US women's national team had never won either event before they broke through in the world championships in 2014. Setter Alisha Glass was a huge reason that Team USA won the world title. She was named the tournament's top setter. Later that year she won the USA Volleyball Female Indoor Athlete of the Year Award for the second straight year. In 2016 she was named the best setter at a tournament the United States won to qualify for the 2016 Olympics.

Dalhausser keeps his eyes on the ball when setting.

But he knows setting is important. It's tough to execute a powerful spike without a good set. So Dalhausser practiced his setting a lot. He was named the top setter on the beach tour six times between 2009 and 2015.

Every player needs to know how to set a ball. Teams usually have a player who plays the position of setter. But if the setter cannot get to a ball, someone else needs to set it.

There are two basic types of sets: a bump set and an overhead set. The bump set is just like a forearm pass. It is a "set" if it is the pass before an attack. A bump set is used when you're unable to get in position for an overhead set.

An overhead set means you pass the ball with your hands, but just the fingertips. The ball cannot stay in your fingertips for more than a split second. And you must touch it with both hands at the same time. Advanced players use overhead sets because they are more accurate.

In 2010 Dalhausser was named the tour's Most Outstanding Player, Best Offensive Player, Best Hitter, Best Blocker, and Best Setter.

DRILL DOWN!

Use this version of target practice to improve your setting skills.

1. Set up three targets, such as cones or tape marks, on one side of the net. The targets should be on the ground about three feet from the net.

2. Have a partner toss a ball to you. Perform a bump set to have the ball land on one of the targets.

3. Continue until you hit each target 10 times.

4. Repeat the process using an overhead set.

SPIKE LIKE

MATT ANDERSON

Matt Anderson loves the big moments. He likes to be the player who scores the key point when his team needs it most.

In the 2015 World Cup, the US men's national team was losing to Italy in the third set. The Americans had won the first two sets, but they needed one more set to clinch the match. Italy was leading 27–26. Games typically go to 25 points, but a team has to win by two.

At 25 years old, Anderson was the youngest member of the US men's volleyball team during the 2012 Olympics.

Team USA needed a point. So as the team received a serve, setter Micah Christenson looked at his options. He faced the left side of the court. But he set the ball behind him while Anderson began running down the right side.

Matt Anderson hits one down the line against Brazil in 2015.

Anderson's spot in the rotation was in the back row. The rules forbid back-row players from hitting in front of the attack line. Christenson knew this and placed the ball perfectly for Anderson.

Anderson had begun his approach in the back-right corner of the court before the setter even touched the ball. When the ball headed his way, he took two more big steps. Anderson then jumped just before he reached the attack line.

SPIKE LIKE MATT ANDERSON

- Watch your footwork. Jump off both feet. Right-handed hitters should have the left foot ahead of the right. This turns your body so you can swing with your right arm.

- Keep your opponents guessing by mixing in offspeed hits, such as a roll shot. Act like you're about to spike, but ease up at the last second and gently hit the ball with an open palm. That action will roll the ball over or around the blockers.

- Another offspeed hit is an open-handed tip. Contact the ball with the pads of your fingertips and send it just over the blockers' hands.

Anderson gets full extension on this spike.

The ball came down a few feet in front of the line. Anderson's momentum carried him forward. At the height of his jump, he spiked the ball with his right hand. It zoomed right past two blockers. An Italian player in the back row stuck out his arm, but the ball bounced off him and skittered away out of bounds.

|||||||||| Anderson was named the USA Volleyball Men's Indoor Player of the Year each year from 2012 to 2015.

That point tied the game. The United States then won the next two points to win the match. The victory kept the

KARCH KIRALY

Karch Kiraly is a volleyball legend. He could do it all—hit, pass, and play defense. He was the first volleyball player to win three Olympic gold medals. His first gold was with the US men's indoor national team in 1984. Kiraly was the youngest on the team. His second medal came in 1988. He was the US team captain and had 137 kills in the tournament. His third was in 1996 in the first Olympic beach volleyball competition. In his career, Kiraly was named the Association of Volleyball Professionals (AVP) Tour's Best Offensive Player three times and the AVP's MVP six times.

A big spike fires up Anderson and his teammates.

Americans undefeated. Italy went on to take second place. Team USA won the tournament. Both teams qualified for the 2016 Olympics.

Anderson was named the tournament's MVP. He led his team in scoring with 172 points in 11 matches. He scored 137 of those points on spikes. That was no surprise. Anderson led the US men's national team in scoring every year from 2011 to 2015.

In the 2016 Olympics in Rio de Janeiro, Brazil, Italy got its revenge with a 3-2 victory over Team USA in the semifinals. However, the Americans rallied from two sets down in the bronze-medal match to beat Russia. Anderson buried a back-row spike for the final point of the match. He ended the Games with 128 points in eight matches, second best among all players in Rio.

Anderson has played professional volleyball in Russia, Italy, and South Korea.

DRILL DOWN!

To practice spiking, all you need is a ball and a wall.

1. Stand about 10 feet away from the wall and toss the ball straight up.

2. Swing your arm over your head and spike the ball downward at a 45-degree angle. A good spike will hit the ground, bounce off the wall, and come right back to you.

3. More advanced players can try spiking while at the top of a jump. Or you can have a friend toss or pass you a ball and spike it over the net.

BLOCK LIKE

KERRI WALSH JENNINGS

The score was tied 8–8 in the second game of the 2012 Olympic beach volleyball gold-medal match. Kerri Walsh Jennings and Misty May-Treanor were the defending champions. But they faced a tough challenge from fellow Americans April Ross and Jennifer Kessy.

Walsh Jennings received a serve. May-Treanor used the second hit to bump a set to her partner in the middle of the court. But Kessy blocked Walsh Jennings' spike. Walsh Jennings doesn't like getting blocked. It only inspires her to return the favor to her opponent.

Walsh Jennings played indoor volleyball at the 2000 Olympics before winning three gold medals in beach volleyball.

Walsh Jennings and May-Treanor fought back to take the lead. Eventually they stretched the lead to four points. That's when Walsh

Kerri Walsh Jennings, *right*, goes up for a block in the 2016 Olympics.

Jennings got her payback for the block. She stood at the net as May-Treanor served to Ross. The pass went to Kessy, who bump-set it back. Walsh Jennings watched the ball the entire time. She shuffled her feet to her right. She planted her feet when she determined she had reached the right spot.

BLOCK LIKE KERRI WALSH JENNINGS

- Footwork is key to getting in position to block. If you need to travel only a few feet right or left, shuffle your feet. If you need to move farther, take a crossover step.

- As you move, keep your hands in front of you and above your waist so it's easier to shoot them above your head when the time comes to jump.

- You should be at the peak of your block jump—with your hands above the net as far as you can reach—just before the opposing hitter contacts the ball.

- Remember that players are not allowed to the touch the net. As a blocker, you want to be as close to the net as you can, but far enough off so your arms won't hit it when you leap up or extend your arms forward during the block.

At 6-foot-2 (188 cm) Walsh Jennings can get high above the net to make a block.

||||||||| Walsh Jennings has been named the best blocker on the beach tour seven times.

She squatted down and jumped up as the ball began to come down. At the top of her leap, with both arms extended straight up, Walsh Jennings leaned to her left. She moved to the spot exactly where Ross tried to spike the ball. Walsh Jennings's hands stopped it from crossing the net. Her block basically sealed the match. Two plays later, the gold medal belonged to her and May-Treanor.

The victory made Walsh Jennings and May-Treanor the first players to win three Olympic beach volleyball medals. They were all gold—a feat that will be tough to match.

CRAIG BUCK

Craig Buck was an intimidating presence on the volleyball court. The middle blocker stood 6 feet 9 inches (206 cm) tall and was an unavoidable obstacle at the net for opposing hitters. Buck was a two-time all-America pick at Pepperdine University and led Team USA to gold medals at the 1984 and 1988 Olympic Games. He was inducted into the International Volleyball Hall of Fame in 1998.

Walsh Jennings blocks a shot against China during the 2016 Olympics.

Rio2016

Walsh Jennings has won more than 600 matches on the beach tour.

Walsh Jennings and May-Treanor didn't lose a match in three Olympic tournaments together.

Later in 2012 Walsh Jennings was named the beach volleyball world tour's Best Blocker. It marked the sixth time she earned that honor. And then she won the title again in 2014. Walsh Jennings might be the best blocker in the history of women's beach volleyball.

Blocking is a skill that takes anticipation, timing, and jumping ability. A skilled blocker is helpful to a volleyball team's success. However, most young players are unable to jump and reach their hands above the net. Blocking becomes a bigger part of the game as players get older.

But young players can begin practicing proper blocking footwork. A good blocker needs her body square to the net when she jumps. This positioning is difficult because she has to move left or right depending on where the ball is. So good footwork helps a blocker get in position.

DRILL DOWN!

Use this drill to develop precise footwork.

1. Stand at the net facing your partner on the other side.

2. Your partner should call out "slide step" or "crossover" and then point either right or left. This direction tells you what to do.

3. Finish each move by facing the net and jumping. After three slide steps or after the big crossover step, jump up and extend your hands above your head.

4. When both players have done each technique 10 times, switch roles.

GLOSSARY

ACE

A serve that lands in the opponent's court, scoring a point for the serving team.

APPROACH

The movements a player makes prior to jumping and hitting the ball.

ATTACK

When a player tries to score a point by hitting the ball over the net toward the opponent.

ATTACK LINE

A line on the floor that runs parallel to the center and end lines on both sides of the court. It is 3 meters (almost 10 feet) from the net and separates each side into a front zone and back zone.

BUMP

To pass the ball by using the forearms with the hands together.

FLOAT SERVE

A served ball that shows little to no spin, making its flight path unpredictable.

LIBERO

A ball-control specialist who plays only in the back row and wears a different colored jersey.

MATCH

An entire volleyball contest, which is made up of three to five sets or games. The first team to win three sets is the winner of the match.

RALLY

The series of actions two teams make to keep the ball in play. When a rally ends, one team is awarded a point.

SPIKE

A hard-driven ball from a player's overhead swing that lands in the opponent's court.

FOR MORE INFORMATION

BOOKS

Abramovitz, Melissa. *Volleyball*. Detroit, MI: Lucent Books, 2013.

Bodden, Valerie. *Volleyball*. Mankato, MN: Creative Education, 2016.

Forest, Anne. *Girls Play Volleyball*. New York: PowerKids Press, 2016.

WEBSITES

To learn more about volleyball, visit **booklinks.abdopublishing.com**. These links are routinely monitored and updated to provide the most current information available.

PLACE TO VISIT

Volleyball Hall of Fame
444 Dwight Street
Holyoke, Massachusetts 01040
(413) 536-0926
www.volleyhall.org
Learn about the greatest athletes ever to play the game of volleyball—in the town where the game started. The Volleyball Hall of Fame opened in 1987, and its first inductee was the late William G. Morgan, the inventor of volleyball. The hall serves as a living memorial to the sport.

INDEX

ABOUT THE AUTHOR

Jon Ackerman has covered six Olympics for NBCOlympics.com. Indoor and beach volleyball were among his assigned sports leading up to the 2008 and 2012 Games. In Beijing and London, he was on-site at the beach volleyball venue. His volleyball writing has also appeared in *Volleyball Magazine,* ESPN.com, UniversalSports.com, and FloVolleyball.tv. He lives in Denver with his wife and daughter.